HELP ME I'VE FALLEN
And I Can't Get Up

T.D. Jakes

DESTINY IMAGE® PUBLISHERS, INC.
P.O. Box 310, Shippensburg, PA 17257-0310

"Speaking to the Purposes of God for this Generation and for the Generations to Come."

This book and all other Destiny Image, Revival Press, Mercy Place, Fresh Bread, Destiny Image Fiction, and Treasure House books are available at Christian bookstores and distributors worldwide.

For a U.S. bookstore nearest you, call 1-800-722-6774.
For more information on foreign distributors, call 717-532-3040.
Or reach us on the Internet: www.destinyimage.com.

ISBN 10: 0-7684-2644-8
ISBN 13: 978-0-7684-2644-1

Previously Published As ISBN 1-56229-435-0

For Worldwide Distribution, Printed in the U.S.A.
7 8 9 10 11 /11 10 09

HELP ME I'VE FALLEN
And I Can't Get Up

Table of Contents

Foreword

I cannot think of a greater living example of the consistent ability to draw on the anointing of the Lord. T.D. Jakes is man without equal. There is much we can all learn from his words, his spirit and his passion in delivering the word of the Lord. Just watching him is a wonder in itself. The Presence of the Lord flows so freely from him as he teaches. He is simple, clear and honest in his delivery. Sometimes urgent, sometimes gentle, but always accurate and penetrating. He is a man whose inner focus is on the Lord Himself. Even in his most emotional presentation, you can also see the rest and peace in his eyes.

The Holy Spirit will always move freely through those who have no other desire than to give the word of the Lord to hungry people. And make no mistake about it, God has much to say to His people. He has much He wants to communicate to the world around us. There is much to learn from the Bishop's words, but also his method, his passion and his love of the Lord Jesus Himself.

I first met the Bishop at a small conference in the Pocono mountains where he was ministering. That was just before he wrote *Woman Thou Art Loosed*. We literally walked into each other that fateful afternoon in the basement area of the conference center where vendors were displaying their products. The moment I touched him I prophesied about a book churning in his heart. A few weeks later he called me and the rest, as they say, is history.

There are three criteria we use when determining the possibility of publishing a new author. We look at the person, his message and his ministry. In the Bishop's case, all three were intricately wrapped with integrity, gentleness and truth. We are proud to offer this work to the world. He is a man who has allowed the Lord to mold him into a vessel He can use to change the lives of millions around the world. We are grateful to be a part of God's plan for the life of Bishop T.D. Jakes.

Don Nori, Publisher

Destiny Image Publishers

Introduction

A popular television commercial for a medical alert device featured an elderly woman who cried out, "Help! I've fallen, and I can't get up!"

The woman wanted to get up but couldn't. Lacking the strength to get back on her feet, she needed help.

As Christians, we all fall from time to time. Life knocks us off balance, lays us low, and renders us weak and incapacitated through no fault of our own. Something inside of us wants to stand, but we don't have the mobility or freedom to act on what we have decided to do.

The cause of the fall is not as important as what we do while we are down. Like the woman in the commercial, we must put aside fear, pride, or embarrassment and learn not only how to ask for help but Whom to ask. After all, help is just a breath away.

Chapter 1
What Comes Before a Fall?

What Comes Before a Fall?

*P*ride comes before destruction and a haughty spirit before a fall (Proverbs 16:18).

Pride comes before a fall. But what is pride? Pride is defined as "being high-minded; showing one's self above others." Another definition states: "Pride is a conceited sense of one's superiority." Pride has caused the fall of many great and gifted individuals.

> *Pride has caused the fall of many great and gifted individuals.*

When Self is Your God

The first known instance of pride occurred before the creation of the earth. Lucifer, the head angel in charge of praise, decided he was going to be greater than God Himself.

How art thou fallen from Heaven, O Lucifer, son of the morning! how art thou cut down to the ground, which didst weaken the nations! For thou hast said in thine heart, I will ascend into Heaven, I will exalt my throne above the stars of God: I will sit also upon the mount of the congregation, in the sides farthest of the north.... I will be like the most High (Isaiah 14:12-14).

Driven by self-deception, prideful self-delusion, and self-importance, Lucifer considered himself better than God. This explains why most of his statements begin with the word *"I"*.

Lucifer, whose name at one time meant "light-bearer," was cast down by God to earth, where he would be known as satan. No longer a praise leader or a majestic angel, instead he became one who roams to and fro on the earth like a lion looking for someone to devour.

Satan's pride led to his downfall. Pride and selfishness go hand in hand. Usually where there is pride, there is also the prevailing spirit of selfishness. Selfishness is defined as "loving one's self first."

Satan thought he could be better than God Himself. Of course he was wrong. satan was deceived. How he even conceived such a thought is beyond imagination. But pride blinds us to the truth and prevents the proud from viewing life realistically.

> *Pride blinds us to the truth and prevents the proud from viewing life realistically.*

As we know, satan has never repented. Instead, he tries to deceive as many of God's children as possible and drag them down to share in his dreadful fallen state.

A Dangerous Place

The prophet Daniel records the downfall of the great Babylonian king, Nebuchadnezzar. One day, the king looked around at all he had accomplished and arrogantly stated: "Is not this great Babylon, that I have built for the house of the kingdom by the might of my power, and for the honour of my majesty?" (Daniel 4:30).

While he was still speaking these arrogant words, a voice from Heaven said, "O King Nebuchadnezzar, to thee it is spoken; The kingdom is departed from thee" (vs. 31). That same hour, the once-great king lost his mind and began to act like an animal, eating grass until "his hairs were grown like eagles' feathers, and his nails like birds' claws" (vs. 33).

Nebuchadnezzar took his eyes off God and began to focus on his accomplishments. Forgetting Who had made him great, the king lost touch with reality and denied truth, thinking he was a self-made man who needed no one.

Nebuchadnezzar did not want to give God any of the glory or thanks for the growth and majesty of the kingdom. He felt that everything he owned belonged to him because he had worked for it. Sound familiar?

When put into a place of prominence, many of God's children forget who brought them to that place. This arrogant and prideful attitude has caused many to fall from the pinnacle of success and popularity.

During the 1980s, several nationally known tele-evangelists let their fame and fortune get the best of them. As a result, pride prevented them from acknowledging their need of God. Considering themselves to be beyond reproach—or advice—they let their guards down. Sin entered their lives, eventually destroying their ministries, their families, and their reputations.

When people (especially Christians who are not rooted and grounded in the Word) start acquiring prestige and experiencing monetary prosperity, they often forget that not long ago they had nothing. Before they owned a nice new car, they could barely afford to ride the bus. Before they lived in a nice new home, their family of five lived in a two-bedroom apartment, not sure how they were going to pay the rent. They were living from paycheck to paycheck.

In spite of their lack, they still managed to give God the glory whether it was by word of mouth or by giving in the offering. They knew that God would meet their needs. But once they came into a place of prosperity, they forgot it was God and God alone who blessed them. Now they look to their jobs or their businesses—or even their ministries—as their source. That is a dangerous place to be.

Contentment versus Self-Sufficiency

Where does the slippery slide into delusion begin? With discontent.

Nebuchadnezzar was not content with his increase; he wanted more. The more he was blessed, the more he wanted. His is a clear case of greed and self-sufficiency brought on by self-deception.

Deception is a trap and stronghold that ensnares many, especially those not content with their own present state in life. The Bible instructs us that we must learn to be content in whatever state we find ourselves. The apostle Paul learned that lesson well: "For I have learned, in whatsoever state I am, therewith to be content" (Philippians 4:11b).

This is not to imply that we should be satisfied with being bound by the devil or be content with complacency and mediocrity; thus, not fulfilling the call of God on our lives. Not at all. We are to work to improve ourselves while at the same time remaining totally dependent on God.

Self-sufficiency means to be "sufficient in oneself," and not putting your faith in God's assistance. Contentment, on the other hand, is to know with certainty and absolute firm conviction that God is able to meet your every need; that

He, Jehovah, is your all sufficiency. Contentment means that you are aware that you don't covet another person's position, property, possessions, or personality. Why? Because you know and are assured that all you presently have and all that you are today is more than enough in the hands of God. Whatever you need to do to fulfill God's purpose you can do—not in your own strength—but through the strength and power of Christ that dwells within your innermost being.

> *Contentment, on the other hand, is to know with certainty and absolute firm conviction that God is able to meet your every need.*

The apostle Paul said, "I know both how to be abased, and I know how to abound: every where and in all things I am instructed both to be full and to be hungry, both to abound and to suffer need. I can do all things through Christ which strengtheneth me" (Philippians 4:12,13).

Where Confusion Reigns

In Nebuchadnezzar's case, the only help for him was repentance. Until he was able to look again to the Father for guidance and to recognize the Lord as his source, he was left in a world of insanity.

You may not enter into a world of insanity like Nebuchadnezzar, but the covering of God will be removed if you allow yourself to fall into an unprotected state.

If you refuse to acknowledge that you have fallen and are separated from God, Who is the eternal source of your supply, you will find yourself in a fallen condition, unable to get up.

Like Nebuchadnezzar, you may refuse to ask for God's help. As a result, confusion will reign in your life.

Nebuchadnezzar's pride and rebellion caused him to lose his kingship until he was willing to acknowledge God.

At the end of the days I Nebuchadnezzar lifted up mine eyes unto Heaven, and mine understanding returned unto me, and I blessed the most High, and I praised and honoured Him that liveth for ever... At the same time my reason returned unto me;...and I was established in my kingdom, and excellent majesty was added unto me. Now I... praise and extol and honour the King of Heaven, all Whose works are truth, and His ways judgment: and those that walk in pride He is able to abase (Daniel 4:34, 36, 37).

Repentance was the key to Nebuchadnezzar's healing and deliverance. When he acknowledged his pride and began to praise and honor God, his mind was restored. But the great king never forgot that God is able to bring low those who "walk in pride."

To fall is bad enough, but to fall and not cry out for help, refusing to repent for your sin, is worse than the fall itself. Some people are so full of pride and consumed with their own self-sufficiency that they think, "If I can't get up myself, I won't let anyone help me."

> *To fall is bad enough, but to fall and not cry out for help, refusing to repent for your sin, is worse than the fall itself.*

Maybe you are ashamed to let anyone know that you have fallen, because you don't want them to think less of you. It is especially difficult to ask for help if you have led people to believe that you are some great, spiritual giant, incapable of falling from your high and lofty place.

Is your image so important that you're willing to continue in your pitiful fallen state? Are you so deceived that you will not acknowledge that you have sinned? Stop being so proud. After all, isn't that what caused you to fall in the first place?

Pride is dangerous because it forces you to lie needlessly in a helpless state for days—and sometimes years. If you had asked for help immediately, you could have gotten up and gone on with your life.

The Way Back

King David began his descent into sin when he lusted for a woman who was not his wife and committed adultery. When Bathsheba became pregnant with his child, David set up her husband to be killed.

The Lord sent Nathan, the prophet of God, to reveal and convict David of his sins:

Wherefore hast thou despised the commandment of the LORD, to do evil in His sight? thou hast killed Uriah the Hittite with the sword, and hast taken his wife to be thy wife, and hast slain him with the sword of the children of Ammon (2 Samuel 12:9).

David, realizing that God knows and sees all things, replied with great sorrow and remorse, "I have sinned against the Lord."

The Lord spared David's life, but the child that he and Bathsheba conceived died.

When David repented of his sins, God picked David up and put him back on his feet.

What if King David had not acknowledged and confessed his sins even after the prophet came to him? What if David had been so full of pride and denial that he would have allowed his kingdom to be destroyed before ever asking God for forgiveness?

Many of you are so bound by pride that you would rather let everything significant be destroyed and diminished by the devil rather than ask God for help. Some people are so prideful that they reject help even when the Lord prompts someone to give it.

We need to be more like David. When we realize we have fallen, we must repent immediately! We need to repent with urgency and sincerity as Kind David did.

Don' t allow satan to deceive you into thinking that because no one saw you commit your sin, you don't have to repent. That deception will cause you to stay in a fallen state. Don't allow pride to lock you into a state of unforgiveness.

> *Don't allow pride to lock you into a state of unforgiveness.*

At times, we fall and are unable to get up or even ask for help. At other times, we have fallen and just do not want to get up and try again because we are afraid we might fall again. Do not stop trying. Like the woman in the medical alert commercial that I mentioned in the introduction, when you've fallen, scream with urgency: "Lord, help! I've fallen, and I can't get up!"

Thoughts and Reflections

_____

_____

_____

_____

_____

_____

_____

_____

_____

_____

_____

_____

_____

_____

_____

_____

_____

_____

_____

_____

_____

_____

_____

_____

_____

What Comes Before a Fall?

_____

_____

_____

_____

_____

_____

_____

_____

_____

_____

_____

_____

_____

_____

_____

_____

_____

_____

_____

_____

_____

_____

_____

Chapter 2
In Your Darkest Hour

In Your Darkest Hour

*T*here is a way which seemeth right
unto a man, but the end thereof are
the ways of death (Proverbs 14:12).

Are you fighting against God? Maybe you
have struggled in your mind, wondering: Should
I ask for help? Who would be willing to help me?
What if they laugh at me? You find yourself trying to get help from everyone except God.

Giving Up the Fight

The apostle Paul, who was formerly named
Saul of Tarsus, had persecuted many Christians

out of religious zeal. He, too, found it hard to accept the fact that he needed help.

> *And as he journeyed, he came near Damascus: and suddenly there shined round about him a light from Heaven: And he fell to the earth, and heard a voice saying unto him, Saul, Saul, why persecutest thou Me? And he said, Who art thou, Lord? And the Lord said, I am Jesus whom thou persecutest: it is hard for thee to kick against the pricks* (Acts 9:3-5).

What did Jesus mean when he said, "I am Jesus whom thou persecutest: it is hard for thee to kick against the pricks"?

The word *"prick"* is the King James translation for the word, "goad." Goad means "to sting; a form of aggressive agitation." Today, we say, "He tried to goad me into a fight."

In this passage from Acts, *"prick"* is used metaphorically to represent the prompting and pricking of the Holy Spirit that God had allowed to come upon Saul's life in an effort to get his attention. The Lord was trying to show Saul that spiritually, he was going down the wrong road and moving in a direction contrary to God's will.

Stubborn and hard-headed, Saul insisted on doing things his own way. After all, he was intelligent, capable, religious—and proud of it! As a result, it took a dramatic move of God to knock Saul off his "high horse."

After being blinded by the bright light, this radical zealot found himself in the humble position of needing someone to lead him by the hand. This temporary loss of sight was God's way of showing Saul there was Someone far greater than he.

God was saying, "Saul, why do you kick against the pricks?" In other words, "Why do you fight against what you know is true? Why do you insist on doing things your own way without first consulting Me?"

Is the Lord asking you the same question, "Why do you kick against the pricks?" The American translation puts it this way, "Why do you allow yourself to continue to run into brick walls?"

These brick walls represent sin and rebellion. Why do we continue to allow satan to deceive us into following him? No matter how sane and rational the sin may seem to you, sin is sin.

Sin always separates us from the presence of God. What a price to pay for wanting things our own way!

> *Sin always separates us from the presence of God.*

In Your Time of Need

Like Saul, we sometimes find ourselves in need of not only divine but human assistance. In fact, God usually sends other people to help us in our time of need.

Blinded for three days, Saul was so depressed he couldn't eat or drink anything. At the same time that Saul thought he had reached his darkest hour, God was preparing a man named Ananias to minister to Saul.

And there was a certain disciple at Damascus, named Ananias; and to him said the Lord in a vision, Ananias. And he said, Behold, I am here, Lord. And the Lord said unto him, Arise, and go into the street which is called Straight, and inquire in the house of Judas for one called Saul, of Tarsus: for, behold, he prayeth, and hath seen in a vision a man named Ananias coming in, and putting his hand on him, that he might receive his sight...

And Ananias went his way, and entered into the house; and putting his hands on him said, Brother Saul, the Lord, even Jesus, that appeared unto thee in the way as thou earnest, hath sent me, that thou mightest receive thy sight, and be filled with the Holy Ghost. And immediately there fell from his eyes as it had been scales: and he received sight forthwith, and arose, and was baptized (Acts 9:10-12,17-18).

If you are in a place where you need God's divine assistance, ask the Lord to send someone to help you. There may already be people in your life who are available to bring healing and deliverance to you. You must, however, be willing to submit, as Saul did, to their ministry. Don't fight divine connections! There is nothing to fear; God will not allow you to be hurt again.

Have you ever noticed the way zoo caretakers handle an injured animal? Even though the caretaker is only interested in helping, the animal does not understand. It only focuses on the pain and, because of this, it will strike or even kill the very person sent to help it.

Some of you may be in this very state. People who have called themselves Christians have done hurtful things to you. You did not expect them to be the ones inflicting the pain. It seemed to hurt far worse because these people professed to love the Lord.

You may have been hurt to such an extent that you no longer trust anybody, not even God. You may not have actually said, "Lord, I don't trust you," but your actions speak louder than words. Maybe you avoid reading God's Word or refuse to allow anyone to pray for you. Do you look for other ways to help alleviate and drown the pain?

God wants to deliver you! He wants to arrest every stronghold and every demonic spirit in your life—every demonic power, every type of sorcery, every hex, every spirit of unbelief, every spirit of doubt, every spirit of pride. God wants you set free, now!

God wants to deliver you!

Profile of the Fallen

What causes someone to fall? Have you experienced something so traumatic and life-changing that you have fallen away from God and forsaken the love of the Father?

Are you one of those saints who was once consumed with doing His will and only His will? Do you now haphazardly serve Him? Were you once preoccupied with spending long hours in conversation with the Lord, but you are now without time to even read His Word? Were you once consumed with the very essence of praise and worship to the Father but now opt to live without praise, except for those times of great need?

Many people fall because they are no longer grafted into the Father. They do not seek His wisdom. Without God's wisdom and the fullness of His Spirit, saints become self-deceived, self-promoting, and just plain carnal and fleshly, thinking only of self. They fool themselves into thinking they can recover by themselves without God's divine intervention or His ordained supernatural human assistance.

Maybe you've given up the fight. Deep in your inner man you have fainted in your spiritual life. You have complained about things you wanted to do but couldn't perform.

God has never said anything that He could not perform. Whether it was, "Let there be light" or "Lazarus come forth", if God said it, He always backed it up by His power and His Spirit.

Before God commissioned Moses to deliver the children of Israel out of Egyptian bondage, He first told him, "I am that I am."

If you're going to continually live a life of victory, the first thing you have got to know is that "God is able."

> *If you're going to continually live a life of victory, the first thing you have got to know is that "God is able."*

"He that cometh to God must believe that He is, and that He is a rewarder of them that diligently seek Him" (Hebrews 11:6).

God says, "Do you not know or at least have you not heard, that I am God, the maker of Heaven and earth and I change not?" In other words, God says, "There is no fainting with Me; there's no failure in Me. I AM THAT I AM."

"God resisteth the proud, but giveth grace unto the humble" (James 4:6).

When you get through searching and trying other things, you're still going to have to come back to God because He holds the power and He has your answer. It is up to you to humble your-self and say, "Lord, help! I've fallen, and I can't get up!"

Struggling in Vain

Have you been living with one foot in and one foot out of God's kingdom, giving God a "maybe," instead of "yes"? If so, it is time to stop struggling. The Holy Ghost is after you; He is in hot pursuit.

The Bible says, "At the name of Jesus every knee shall bow…And that every tongue should confess that Jesus Christ is Lord to the glory of God" (Philippians 2:10, 11). So why wait to be brought to your knees? Acknowledge Jesus as Lord of your life today. It will save you a lot of pain and sorrow.

Have ye not known? have ye not heard? Hath it not been told you from the begin-ning? Have ye not understood from the foundations of the earth? It is He that sit-teth upon the circle of the earth, and the inhabitants thereof are as grasshoppers; that stretcheth out the heavens as a cur-tain, and spreadeth them out as a tent to dwell in: That bringeth the princes to nothing; He maketh the judges of the earth as vanity…To whom then will ye liken Me, or shall I be equal? saith the Holy One. Lift up your eyes on high, and behold Who hath created these things, that bringeth out their host by number: He calleth them all by names by the greatness of His might, for that He is strong in power, not one faileth. Why sayest thou, O Jacob, and speakest, O Israel, My way is hid from the Lord, and my judgment is passed over from my God? Hast thou not known? Hast thou not heard, that the everlasting God, the Lord, the Creator of the ends of the earth, fainteth not, neither is weary? There is no searching of His understanding. He giveth power to the faint; and to them that have no might He increaseth strength. Even the youths shall faint and be weary, and the young men shall utterly fall: But they that wait upon the Lord shall renew their strength; they shall mount up with wings as eagles; they shall run, and not be weary; and they shall walk; and not faint (Isaiah 40:21-23, 25-31).

When your pity party is over and you are ready for His help, God will say, "Don't you know? Have you not heard Who I am—the everlasting God? I am the Creator of the universe. I am not a child; I am not a school boy—I am

God. "Who do you think you're fooling? I'm God. I hold your breath in My hands. I created your body. I heat your blood just hot enough to keep you alive, but not so hot that you die. I'm God. I measured your life in the sands of my own hand. I'm God. "Why would you serve anybody else? Who else do you allow to control your life? If it is not Me, then who? I love you. I created you in My image. I am that I am."

Why do you continue in this fallen state? What more does the Lord have to do or say to show you He loves you? Don't let satan continue to fool you into thinking that God has forsaken you.

Stop blaming others for your mistakes. Realize and admit that there is something wrong with you. Quit being mad at everyone and stop trying to adjust the whole world to fit your circumstances.

When some folks go down, they want to lower the standard for everyone else. They want everything to fit into their world. They want to start calling wrong, right, and calling right, wrong.

Stop doing things that you know you don't have any business doing. Repent and confess your sins instead of spending your time pointing out the sins of everyone else. Admit that you have fallen so that your healing may begin.

> *Admit that you have fallen so that your healing may begin.*

Stop running into those brick walls. Die to your pride and ask for help! He will help you and restore you to your former state. Just ask for help. Let your heart be opened to God. He will be there for you, even in your darkest hour.

Thoughts and Reflections

_____

_____

_____

_____

_____

_____

_____

_____

_____

_____

_____

_____

_____

_____

_____

_____

_____

_____

_____

_____

_____

_____

_____

_____

_____

_____

_____

_____

_____

_____

_____

_____

_____

_____

_____

_____

_____

_____

_____

_____

_____

_____

_____

_____

_____

_____

_____

_____

_____

Chapter 3
Getting Back on Track

Getting Back on Track

*W*herefore let him that thinketh he standeth take heed lest he fall (1 Corinthians 10:12).

You may have heard the story about the misbehaving little boy whose mother told him to sit in the corner chair. "I may be sitting on the outside," he said, "but I'm standing on the inside."

That's the way many adults act when they rebel against God. Standing in our own strength, however, puts us most in danger of falling. When we think we are strong, we are easy prey for the devil.

> *When we think we are strong, we are easy prey for the devil.*

Between the Devil and the Deep Blue Sea

The prophet Jonah did not want to do what he knew he was called to do. Instead, he murmured and complained and then tried to run. We can't run from God, but we can run out from the protection of the Lord.

That is what Jonah did, but God didn't stop chasing him. He caused a fish to swallow him.

While in the belly of the great fish, Jonah said, "I've messed up. I've blown it. I've goofed. I've gotten into trouble. I've gotten myself in a mess." Jonah realized he had fallen, and he was now in a place where he had to repent of his rebellion.

Then Jonah prayed unto the Lord his God out of the fish's belly, And said, I cried by reason of mine affliction unto the Lord, and He heard me; out of the belly of hell cried I, and thou heardest my voice. For thou hadst cast me into the deep, in the midst of the seas; and the floods compassed me about: all thy billows and thy waves passed over me. Then I said, I am cast out of thy sight; yet I will look again toward thy holy temple (Jonah 2:1-4).

Notice how Jonah's emotions wavered. At one moment, Jonah was calling on God, but then doubt rose up in his heart and he said, "I am cast out of God's sight."

Has the devil ever told you, "God is not even thinking about you; God can't see you; God doesn't love you anymore; He doesn't care about you; after all, you sinned"?

In the midst of Jonah's feeble prayer, the thought popped up: "I'm too far gone, and I'm cast out of His sight."

Have you ever had to pray with fear in your heart and uncertainty in your spirit not knowing in your own mind whether God could hear you or not?

God is not deaf, nor is He hard of hearing. God is not like Grandpa; He's God. He can hear your thoughts afar off. He can hear a snake running through the grass in the middle of a rain storm. He knows what you are trying to say even before you say it.

> *God is not deaf, nor is*
> *He hard of hearing.*

God will raise you up if you ask Him. Like Jonah, you don't have to do anything special to get God's attention. All He asks is that you humble yourself. God wants you to be delivered out of your desperate situation, but it is up to you not to resist the Holy Ghost. Submit humbly to God; resist the devil and the devil will flee from you. First, you must submit—as Jonah did—to God and His will for your life.

> *He knows what you are trying*
> *to say even before you say it.*

Going Around in Circles

It takes more than just saying you submit to God. You have to walk it out day by day trusting Him to lead and guide you into deliverance and fulfillment. If you don't, you will only end up going around in circles.

After the children of Israel were freed from Egyptian bondage, they spent the majority of their time complaining about their circumstances. Rather than thanking God for His miraculous deliverance, they murmured and griped constantly about their living conditions.

As a result, an eleven-day journey to Canaan took forty years. The children of Israel wandered around in the wilderness until all of the original complainers died off.

They forgat God their savior, which had done great things in Egypt; Wondrous works in the land of Ham, and terrible things by the Red sea. Therefore He said that He would destroy them, had not Moses His chosen stood before Him in the breach, to turn away His wrath, lest He should destroy them. Yea, they despised the pleasant land, they believed not His word: But murmured in their tents, and hearkened not unto the voice of the LORD. Therefore He lifted up His hand against them, to overthrow them in the wilderness: To overthrow their seed also among the nations, and to scatter them in the lands (Psalm 106:21-27).

The doubters and complainers could not enter into God's place of peace and tranquillity because of unbelief.

God had tolerated, as long as He could, the people's ungratefulness to Him for bringing them out of 400 years of hard, cruel Egyptian slavery and bondage. God had taken all He was going to of their whining and crying, like little spoiled babies, because they couldn't get their way.

He fed them meals day and night; He provided them with free lights—the sun by day and a pillar of fire by night. God put clothes on their backs and shoes on their feet, neither of which ever wore out or grew old. But through all of this, they were not content and failed to show or express to God any gratitude or thankfulness. All they did was complain, complain, and complain.

Frustrating God's Grace

The Israelites' grumbling and complaining was not what finally frustrated God's tolerance. Their immature behavior simply exemplified the condition of their hearts.

What really displeased God was their failure to walk by faith—their evil hearts of unbelief. "Take heed, brethren, lest there be in any of you an evil heart of unbelief, in departing from the living God" (Hebrews 3:12). A hard heart provokes God more than anything else.

> *A hard heart provokes God more than anything else.*

While it is said, Today if ye will hear His voice, harden not your hearts, as in the provocation. For some, when they had heard, did provoke: howbeit not all that came out of Egypt by Moses. But with whom was he grieved forty years? Was it not with them that had sinned, whose carcases fell in the wilderness? And to whom sware He that they should not enter into his rest, but to them that believed not? (Hebrews 3:18).

When you do not trust in God's goodness and walk in unbelief, you frustrate the generous grace of God. The apostle Paul wrote, "*I* do not frustrate the grace of God: for if righteousness comes by the law, then Christ is dead in vain" (Galatians 2:21).

I warn you, brother and sister, do not frustrate the grace of God as the Israelites did. The Bible says that God will not always strive with man. God is merciful, longsuffering and forgiving, but that does not absolve or excuse us from yielding to the Spirit so that we may be empowered to take responsibility for our own salvation.

> *Wherefore, My beloved, as ye have always obeyed, not as in My presence only, but now much more in My absence, work out your own salvation with fear and trembling. For it is God which worketh in you both to will and to do of His good pleasure* (Philippians 2:12-13).

We are without excuse, for God has given us everything we need for eternal life and godliness. Why insist on doing things your own way? Submit to God and He will give you the power to overcome every obstacle in your life, one by one.

Submit to God and He will give you the power to overcome every obstacle in your life.

Religion can't help you. Trying to abide by legalistic church traditions won't help you out of your situation. The only source guaranteed to pull you through, every time you ask, is God Almighty.

Our Heavenly Defense Attorney

What was God's purpose for taking the Israelites through the wilderness pathway? He wanted to develop their faith in His goodness and in His ability and willingness to help them. God wanted them to know that He would care for and protect them and meet their every need regardless of the circumstances or the situations at hand.

They failed to get the picture. As a result, many were destroyed by snake bites, earthquakes, and various plagues. God would have killed them all; but Moses, who was the friend of God, gained a reprieve by pleading their case before God.

We no longer have Moses today, but as born-again citizens of the Kingdom of God, we have an Advocate who sits at the right hand of the Father constantly making intercession for the saints of Almighty God. His name is Jesus.

"Wherefore He is able also to save them to the uttermost that come unto God by Him, seeing He ever liveth to make intercession for them" (Hebrews 7:25).

Before God will let you go under, He will take you over. In the meantime, you will experience "struggling time." Your faith has to be tried. And when your faith is being tested, all hell breaks loose.

> *Before God will let you go under, He will take you over.*

During times of tribulation, demons begin to attack your faith. Satan brings false accusations against you during the trial of your faith. Principalities bring condemning indictments, but you cannot lose with the lawyer I use. Jesus has never lost a case.

The Word of God declares, "If we say that we have not sinned, we make Him a liar, and His Word is not in us" (1 John 1:10). But the Word of God also goes on to say that if anyone does sin, "we have an advocate with the Father, Jesus Christ the righteous" (1 John 2:1b).

Jesus Christ is our constant advocate and our high priest before God:

> *Seeing then that we have a great High Priest, that is passed into the heavens, Jesus the Son of God, let us hold fast our profession. For we have not an high priest which cannot be touched with the feeling of our infirmities; but was in all points tempted like as we are, yet without sin* (Hebrews 4:14,15).

Do not allow your situation to lock you into a spirit of delusion and complacency. Remember, the devil is trying to kill you. He wants you dead. Only the Spirit of God and the blood of Jesus stand between you and destruction. Do not let satan deceive you into thinking that no one cares or that God has not heard your cries for help.

God knows your moanings and your groanings. God knows what your tears mean when they well up in your eyes. If you call on Him, He will answer you. Trust Him. If He said He will bring you through, He will.

Quit complaining about your situation. Ask God to help you, put away your pride and just ask for help. Do not allow pride to keep you immobilized in your fallen state.

Something in you has got to cry, "Lord, help! I've fallen, and I can't get up! I don't like the way I'm living; I don't like the way I'm hurting. Something in me needs to change. Something in me needs to be broken. I need to be set free by the power of God."

All you have to do is ask. God says, "ask, and it shall be given you; seek, and ye shall find; knock, and it shall be opened unto you" (Matthew 7:7).

Remember, you have a High Priest who has made it possible for you to come boldly before the throne of grace to seek help in your time of need. When you seek God with your whole heart, you will find Him.

> *When you seek God with your whole heart, you will find Him.*

Thoughts and Reflections

_____

_____

_____

_____

_____

_____

_____

_____

_____

_____

_____

_____

_____

_____

_____

_____

_____

_____

_____

_____

_____

_____

_____

_____

_____

_____

_____

_____

_____

_____

_____

_____

_____

_____

_____

_____

_____

_____

_____

_____

_____

_____

_____

_____

_____

_____

_____

Chapter 4
Healing For Past Hurts

Healing For Past Hurts

*T*he steps of a good man are ordered by the Lord; and He delighteth in his way. Though he fall, he shall not be utterly cast down: for the Lord upholdeth him with His hand (Psalm 37:23-24).

Has something so painful and overwhelming happened to you that it has affected every area of your life? Every time you kneel to pray, does your mind go back to the fact that someone broke your heart and wounded your spirit?

Have you experienced something so personally devastating that you can't discuss it with anyone? You find it difficult to trust people, and you don't know where to turn. You may feel as if everyone is grading you and evaluating your progress—when actually you are your own harshest judge.

You know you should be further along in life, but someone or some circumstance crippled your faith. Your hopes and dreams were never fulfilled.

You know you should have finished school; you know you should have been a teacher or a musician by now. By society's standards, you should already be married and have children. Maybe you think your ministry should be further along or that you should have a successful career at this point in your life. Your dreams and goals should have been fulfilled years ago, but you've been crippled.

Don't give up. There is hope for you and healing for past hurts.

Dreams Fulfilled

Joseph had dreams. It took years, however, for those dreams to be fulfilled. In spite of the tragedies in his life, Joseph never let go of the dreams God had given him.

Now Israel loved Joseph more than all his children, because he was the son of his old age: and he made him a coat of many colours. And when his brethren saw that their father loved him more than all his brethren, they hated him, and could not speak peaceably unto him. And Joseph dreamed a dream, and he told it his brethren: and they hated him yet the more (Genesis 37:3-5).

On the outside, Joseph was a have-not, rejected and despised by his own brothers. God had plans for Joseph long before he was ever sold into slavery. From the circumstances, however, that fact didn't always appear to be true. Nevertheless, God had His hand on Joseph's life.

While in slavery and in prison, Joseph was not experiencing conditions that indicated he was going to be successful. He didn't look like a man marked to be a great leader, but he was.

And the LORD was with Joseph, and he was a prosperous man; and he was in the house of his master the Egyptian. And his master saw that the LORD was with him, and that the LORD made all that he did to prosper in his hand...The keeper of the prison looked not to any thing that was under his hand; because the LORD was with him, and that which he did, the LORD made it to prosper (Genesis 39:2-3, 23).

God, however, has a way of taking people who have been forsaken by men and raising them up. In fact, God tends to prefer such individuals because, when they get into a place of power, they are not arrogant like those who think they deserve to be promoted.

Egypt's Pharaoh recognized these qualities in Joseph and exalted him to the highest position in the nation.

And Pharaoh said unto his servants, Can we find such a one as this is, a man in whom the spirit of God is? And Pharaoh said unto Joseph, Forasmuch as God hath shown thee all this, there is none so discreet and wise as thou art: Thou shalt be over my house, and according unto thy word shall all my people be ruled: only in the throne will I be greater than thou. And Pharaoh said unto Joseph, See, I have set thee over all the land of Egypt (Genesis 41:38-41).

Broken individuals tend not to be quite so self-righteous. They tend to be a little warmer and more loving, reaching out to embrace others without fear of rejection. They understand that if it had not been for the Lord, they wouldn't be who they are. They realize that if it had not been for God's grace and mercy, they would have never survived.

Joseph exhibited these qualities in the way he treated his once-hateful brothers. When he revealed himself, instead of condemning them for their act of violence against him, Joseph forgave his brothers.

And Joseph said unto his brethren, Come near to me, I pray you. And they came near. And he said, I am Joseph your brother, whom ye sold into Egypt. Now therefore be not grieved, nor angry with yourselves, that ye sold me hither: for God did send me before you to preserve life. For these two years hath the famine been in the land: and yet there are five years, in the which there shall neither be earing nor harvest. And God sent me before you to preserve you a posterity in the earth, and to save your lives by a great deliverance. So now it was not you that sent me hither, but God: and He hath made me a father to Pharaoh, and lord of all his house, and a ruler throughout all the land of Egypt (Genesis 45:4-8).

Joseph did not blame God for his former troubles, instead he realized that God's hand had been on his life all along.

Healed to Help Others

God has a way of bringing us out of bondage and then making us remember where we came from. When we—like Joseph—begin to experience success and victory, God will remind us that He opened the door of the prison. He set us free. He gave us favor in the eyes of men. Now it is our turn to bless others. When God raises you up, you'll have more compassion for other people. You'll look for people you can help.

The church needs healed and delivered Christians who are willing to be used by God to bless others. God is looking for people who have enough compassion to stop and ask, "How are you today?" and then stay long enough to hear the answer.

Instead of always expecting someone to bless you, be moved to help a brother or sister in need. It was God's grace and mercy that allowed you to survive the situation that crippled you. Now it is your responsibility to remember and encourage those who may be experiencing a similar problem.

When people have been wounded and crippled by the circumstances of life, they need special care, extra attention, and unconditional love. They have to be held a little closer and prayed over a little longer because their trust has been broken and betrayed.

They may have been told by well-meaning friends, "I'm going to be there for you." Others have said, "You can depend one me." But they lied.

I know pastors who trusted and depended on fellow associates only to be betrayed and stabbed in the back. Now these pastors are crippled and unable to minister.

I also know church people who have been disillusioned by pastors who used them and then discarded them like an old worn-out shirt. As a result, these wounded workers walk with a limp, crippled by unforgiveness and fear.

No one is exempt from being crippled, but everyone can be healed if they allow the Lord to shoulder all of their past hurts and tear down the walls of unforgiveness. Unforgiveness is a stronghold that sets up residence in the heart. It causes you to be hard-hearted, angry, and bitter toward others and even toward God!

If you forgive those who have hurt you, the Holy Spirit can bring healing. He will come to you and say "You are hurting, but you're going to make it. You've been wounded, but I'm going to help you. I know you've got a weak side, but I'm going to strengthen you. I know you don't have a lot of help, but I'm going to be your support. I know you have been abandoned, but I'm going to stand by you."

If you forgive those who have hurt you, the Holy Spirit can bring healing.

What Only You Can Do

You may have asked "How can a perfect God have a crippled child?" God specializes in taking those who have been broken and neglected by others and restoring them. God says, "I take little and create much."

> *God says, "I take little and create much."*

You have more potential than you think. You can achieve much more than people expect of you. You can go as far in life as your faith will take you.

They said you won't last, but He can strengthen you. They said God could not use someone like you, but He thinks differently. God sees potential that not even you know is there.

You may be saying to yourself, "I've done so much wrong, I can't get up; I'm so far out that I can't get back in."

The devil is a liar! It does not matter what you have done. It does not matter where you have been. God is a God of second chances. He is the God of new beginnings. When you're down, He'll pick you up again.

When God restores you, it does not matter who is trying to bind you or who is fighting against you. All you need to know is that when God brings you up, no demon in hell can bring you down.

> *When God brings you up,*
> *no demon in hell can*
> *bring you down.*

If God has blessed you, shout it from the housetops! If God brought you up, praise and thank Him! Every time I think about what the Lord has done for me, my soul rejoices.

No one can tell your testimony. No one knows what God has done for you. No one knows how far you've come. No one knows what you've been through. But you know it was only by the grace of God that you survived. Don't allow the devil to steal your testimony.

It may have taken you longer than everybody else, but God has given you the victory. Tell others what God has done in your life. The devil would love for you not to tell your testimony. Why? Because if you tell what

God has done for you, someone else might get set free.

God's Mercy

There is not a person alive today who has not benefitted from God's mercy. It was God's mercy that prevailed in the garden of Eden. When Adam and Eve sinned, the Lord could have scrapped everything and started all over again. God was merciful and allowed Adam and Eve to live with the hope that their seed would redeem back what they had lost.

God's mercy prevailed in the wilderness with Moses and the children of Israel. When the Israelites moaned and groaned, their fate could have ended in immediate and total destruction, but God was merciful.

When Jonah refused to go to Nineveh, God could have killed the unwilling prophet and found another to go in his place. It was God's mercy that allowed the fish to swallow Jonah. God knew what was in Jonah just as He knows what is in you and me.

Sometimes God will allow us to fall because in our time of falling we come to realize that without Him we are nothing. We become convinced that it is only by His mercy that we are able to stand.

"His mercy endureth for ever. Let the redeemed of the Lord say so" (Psalm 107:1,2). This verse reminds me of the song, "Your Grace And Mercy," which simply says:

> Your grace and mercy has
> brought me through,
>
> And I'm living this moment
> because of you.
>
> I want to thank you and
> praise you, too;
>
> Your grace and mercy has
> brought me through.

God's grace and mercy has brought you through. Quit acting as if you have made it on your own. Stop pretending you're here because you're so good. The devil is a liar, and he would have you deceived into thinking your deliverance was and is by some act or power of your own.

"O give thanks unto the Lord, for He is good: for His mercy endureth for ever" (Psalm 107:1).

God's Sufficient Grace

The apostle Paul wrote, "And He said unto me, My grace is suff<!---->icent for thee: for my strength is made perfect in weakness" (2 Cor. 12:9).

When we are asking and believing God for something, it may take time for it to become a reality in our lives. As a result, the spirit of discouragement attempts to latch onto us and drag us down, saying, "You're not going to get it. You're not going to get up. You're not going to be free. You're not going to get out. You're not going to be loosed. You're not going to be happy, and you're not going to have joy. You're not ever going to be satisfied. You're going to die frustrated. You're going to end up depressed and discouraged."

The devil is a liar. He wants us to think there is no help in God and no balm in Gilead. God may not come when you want Him to come, but He's always right on time—if you wait on Him.

"For the Lord God is a sun and shield: the Lord will give grace and glory: no good thing will He withhold from them that walk uprightly" (Psalm 84:11).

Whatever God declares or decrees, He has the power to perform. He has never yet said anything that He couldn't back up. He has never claimed to be able to do anything that He could not do.

Never be in a position where you are too good or too busy to ask God for help. Never get to a point where you think you can make it on your own. That is pride at its worst. And before a fall there is pride, and after pride there is destruction.

> *Never be in a position where you are too good or too busy to ask God for help.*

Without God's help, we would all be doomed to lives of pain and self-destruction. When I have been desperate and afflicted, I knew it was the power of the Holy Spirit that carried me and rescued me.

We cannot do anything without God. We can't breathe without God. We can't think without God. We can't even get up without God.

Don't let satan deceive you into believing that you can make it on your own. As soon as you fall, satan is right there whispering, "You will never get up."

But you can call on God for help and realize that He is always "at Hand... and not a God afar off" (Jeremiah 23:23).

> *Don't let satan deceive you into believing that you can make it on your own.*

Thoughts and Reflections

_____

_____

_____

_____

_____

_____

_____

_____

_____

_____

_____

_____

_____

_____

_____

_____

_____

_____

_____

_____

_____

_____

_____

_____

_____

_____
_____
_____
_____
_____
_____
_____
_____
_____
_____
_____
_____
_____
_____
_____
_____
_____
_____
_____
_____
_____
_____
_____
_____

Chapter 5
Strength to Stand

Strength to Stand

Who art thou that judgest another man's servant? To his own master he standeth or falleth. Yea, he shall be holden up: for God is able to make him stand (Romans 14:4).

Do you believe God is able to pick you up and make you stand? Until you know that God is able, you will never cry out for help.

God asked the prophet Isaiah, "Hast thou not known? hast thou not heard, that the everlasting God, the Lord, the Creator of the ends of the earth, fainteth not, neither is weary?" (Isaiah 40:28a).

God wants us to understand that there is no lack of strength in Him. You may not have much of a prayer life, but God says, "Has thou not known?" In other words, you should have known that He would take care of you.

The Word says that the everlasting God, me Creator of the universe, is all powerful. He has brought you through many problems, so don't let satan deceive you into thinking that it was just luck or coincidence that delivered you.

Remember what God has done for you. If you can't seem to remember anything He has done for you personally, then look around at others who have been delivered out of situations worse than yours. See what God did for them and tell yourself, "If He can do it for them, I know He can do it for me." God's divine love and power brought them through, and He will do the same for you.

> *Remember what God has done for you.*

God says, "I have the strength that is necessary to escalate and motivate and move you up and out of your circumstances."

They live in rebellion against God's Word, which clearly commands, "Trust in the Lord with all thine heart; and lean not unto thine own understanding. In all thy ways acknowledge Him, and He shall direct thy paths" (Proverbs 3:5,6).

Because of their pride, such people never seek God's counsel on anything or consult the advice of the Word of God on important decisions. When they do go to the Bible about some matter or pressing issue, they misinterpret God's Word to make it mean what they want it to say. They have become very skilled and crafty at erroneously using the Word to rationalize and justify their own selfish motivations.

Remember, "There is a way which seemeth right unto a man, but the end thereof are the ways of death" (Proverbs 14:12).

Instead of traveling this road of destruction, you can take the righteous alternative, which is the counsel of God. If you want to be victorious in all your endeavors, then don't lean on your own understanding or to your own devices or innovations. Instead, in all your ways acknowledge the Lord, and He will direct your path.

Seek the Word of the Lord about everything that concerns you, and you will, like the great warrior Joshua, have good success.

If you want to be profitable in business and successful in life, develop an attitude and habit of inquiring of the Lord and you will never fail. Turn from the wicked way of your own fleshly wisdom and acknowledge the Lord—and He will direct your path. "For as many as are led by the Spirit of God, they are the sons of God" (Romans 8:14).

Renewed Strength

The Bible says that God "giveth power to the faint; and to them that have no might He increaseth strength" (Isaiah 40:29). In other words, He is saying, "I won't kill you because you fainted. I give power to the faint."

When you start losing the strength you once had, you are fainting. When you can hardly stand up, and you begin to stagger in the throws of sin, lust, envy, and strife, God declares, "I give power to the faint!"

God says, "I give power, not to the person who is standing strong, but to the one who is swaying on wobbly knees. I give power to the faint." To those who have no might, He said, "I will increase their strength."

If you have looked inside yourself and cannot muster the strength to get up, God says, "I will increase your strength."

Think back for a moment to the elderly woman in that commercial. She did not only need someone to help her up, but she needed someone or something to make her stronger.

God will not only raise you up, but He'll give you enough power to pull yourself up if you stumble again. He won't help you up so you can be handicapped the rest of your life. No. He gives power to the faint, and to those who are weak He gives strength.

Are you weak with no will-power, no strength, no ability within yourself to resist the enemy? When your body gets tired, remember God and His strength. When satan begins to attack you, remember the power of God residing within your innermost being. Remember that God does not faint or grow weary. In fact, the Holy One does not even sleep.

> *Remember that God does not faint or grow weary.*

When you remember these things about your Father, your strength will suddenly be renewed. Your joy will be restored, and your power will return. You will begin to experience a life of victory.

Waiting on God

God says, "If you wait on Me, I'll renew your strength. If you wait on Me, everything will be all right."

You may be hurt right now, but be patient. Help is on the way.

I know you've cried out, "Lord, help! I've fallen, and I can't get up." The Holy Spirit says, "Wait. Help is on the way. Just hold on, God is coming to your aid. He's coming to deliver you and to set you free."

God is going to bring you out and loose you from your captivity. He's going to renew your strength. If you hold on a little while longer, your change is going to come.

Remember Samson who lost everything; he lost his hair, his strength, and his eyes. Samson lost his position, his family, his wife, and his reputation. He was reduced from a great warrior to grinding at the mill.

But without a doubt, at an appointed time, Samson's strength was renewed.

Samson's attitude was, "Lord, I'm waiting on you. If you don't help me, I'll die without ever being redeemed from the error of my ways. Lord, if you don't help me, I'll never get my honor back. God, if you don't help me, I'll never get up from where I've fallen."

While he was waiting, Samson's strength began to return.

The secret to renewing your strength is waiting on the Lord. God's Word says, "But they that wait upon the Lord shall renew their strength" (Isaiah 40:31a).

At times you may not have been able to explain it or prove it, but you knew you were waiting on something to happen in your life. The devil said, "You need to give up and die," but something inside you said, "Hold out a little while longer."

The devil said, "You're not going to get it," but something else said, "Wait. You're hurting, but wait; you're crying, but wait; you've missed it, but wait on the Lord and everything is going to be all right."

On Eagles' Wings

"They shall mount up on wings as eagles; they shall run, and not be weary; and they shall walk, and not faint" (Isaiah 40:31b).

God declares, "I'll cause your wings to stretch out. You will mount up on wings like eagles. I'll take you above the top of the storm clouds."

The eagle does not fly in the storm; it flies above the storm. Spreading its wings wide, the eagle uses the wind blowing against it to take it higher instead of lower.

You don't have to let the wind bring you down. If you just stretch out on God's Word, the same wind that is trying to take you under will hold you up and take you over into the glory of God.

You're going to walk and not faint, but first you must come to God with your whole heart. Humble yourself and tell the Lord that you're unable to do it alone. Tell the Lord that you've tried, but you can't seem to get the victory—you just can't get up.

"Lord, I've been lying here on the ground of adversity and defeat. I've tried, but I can't get up. The desire is there in my mind and my will, but when I try to get back on my feet, I can't get my flesh to cooperate with what the Word of God says I can do. I'm thinking right, but I'm not doing right. I'm saying the right things, but I can't get up."

It is at this point that you must call out: "Lord, you've got to help me, or I'll never get out of this. Lord, help! I've fallen, and I can't get up! I'm pretending to be stronger than I am, but I need You to renew my strength. God, give me back my will to fight."

You also need to confess: "Lord, I know I'm allowing things in my life that should not be there. I repent of my sin. I want to be delivered, but I continue to be bound. I don't have the strength to deliver myself. I need the Holy Spirit working in my life again."

Brothers and sisters, when your situation gets desperate, you need to run to God like you have never run before and cry out: "Jesus, I'm on the verge of destruction. If you don't help me, the enemy is going to annihilate me. He's about to take me out! Help me, Lord Jesus!"

> *When your situation gets desperate, you need to run to God.*

The Holy Spirit is calling you. Put away the excuses and the complaints. God is calling you. Give Him everything, and allow Him to renew your strength.

The areas of your life that you have not given up to Him, you need to release right now. Don't be bound any longer. The Lord will not renew your strength until you are willing to throw everything on the altar, without restrictions or reservations.

When you've given Him all of you, He'll give you all of Him—no more "some" of you and "some" of Him. It's time in your life that it's "none" of you and "all" of Him.

> *When you've given Him all of you, He'll give you all of Him.*

When you make that decision, He'll enable you to mount up on eagle's wings and soar with the mighty wind of the Spirit.

God will pick you up and make you stand.

Thoughts and Reflections

_____

_____

_____

_____

_____

_____

_____

_____

_____

_____

_____

_____

_____

_____

_____

_____

_____

_____

_____

_____

_____

_____

_____

Strength to Stand

_____

_____

_____

_____

_____

_____

_____

_____

_____

_____

_____

_____

_____

_____

_____

_____

_____

_____

_____

_____

_____

_____

_____

_____

Bonus Material

Infirmed Woman

A nd, behold, there was a woman which had a spirit of infirmity eighteen years, and was bowed together, and could in no wise lift up herself. And when Jesus saw her, He called her to Him, and said unto her, Woman, thou art loosed from thine infirmity (Luke 13:11-12).

The Holy Spirit periodically lets us catch a glimpse of the personal testimony of one of the patients of the Divine Physician Himself. This woman's dilemma is her own, but perhaps you will find some point of relativity between her case history and your own. She could be like someone you know or have known; she could even be like you.

There are three major characters in this story. These characters are the person, the problem and the prescription. It is important to remember that for every person, there will be a problem. Even more importantly, for every problem, our God has a prescription!

> *For every problem, our God has a prescription!*

Jesus' opening statement to the problem in this woman's life is not a recommendation for counseling—it is a challenging command! Often much more is involved in maintaining deliverance than just discussing past trauma. Jesus did not counsel what should have been commanded. I am not, however, against seeking the counsel of godly men. On the contrary, the Scriptures say:

> *Blessed is the man that walketh not in the counsel of the ungodly, nor standeth in the way of sinners, nor sitteth in the seat of the scornful* (Psalm 1:1).

*Where no counsel is, the people fall: but
in the multitude of counsellors there is
safety* (Proverbs 11:14).

What I want to make clear is that after you
have analyzed the condition—after you have understood its origin—it will still take the authority
of God's Word to put the past under your feet!
This woman was suffering as a result of something that attacked her 18 years earlier. I wonder if you can relate to the long-range after-effects
of past pain? This kind of trauma is as fresh to
the victim today as it was the day it occurred. Although the problem may be rooted in the past,
the prescription is a present word from God! The
Word is the same yesterday, today and forever-
more! (See Hebrews 13:8.) That is to say, the
word you are hearing today is able to heal your
yesterday!

> *Although the problem may
> be rooted in the past, the
> prescription is a present
> Word from God!*

Jesus said, "Woman, thou art loosed." He
did not call her by name. He wasn't speaking to
her just as a person. He spoke to her femininity.

He spoke to the song in her. He spoke to the lace in her. Like a crumbling rose, Jesus spoke to what she could, and would, have been. I believe the Lord spoke to the twinkle that existed in her eye when she was a child; to the girlish glow that makeup can never seem to recapture. He spoke to her God-given uniqueness. He spoke to her gender.

Her problem didn't begin suddenly. It had existed in her life for 18 years. We are looking at a woman who had a personal war going on inside her. These struggles must have tainted many other areas of her life. The infirmity that attacked her life was physical. However, many women also wrestle with infirmities in emotional traumas. These infirmities can be just as challenging as a physical affliction. An emotional handicap can create dependency on many different levels. Relationships can become crutches. The infirmed woman then places such weight on people that it stresses a healthy relationship. Many times such emotional handicaps will spawn a series of unhealthy relationships.

For thou hast had five husbands; and he whom thou now hast is not thy husband: in that saidst thou truly (John 4:18).

Healing cannot come to a desperate person rummaging through other people's lives. One of the first things that a hurting person needs to do is break the habit of using other people as a narcotic to numb the dull aching of an inner void. The more you medicate the symptoms, the less chance you have of allowing God to heal you.

> *The more you medicate the symptoms, the less chance you have of allowing God to heal you.*

The other destructive tendency that can exist with any abuse is the person must keep increasing the dosage. Avoid addictive, obsessive relationships. If you are becoming increasingly dependent upon anything other than God to create a sense of wholeness in your life, then you are abusing your relationships.

Clinging to people is far different from loving them. It is not so much a statement of your love for them as it is a crying out of your need for them. Like lust, it is intensely selfish. It is taking and not giving. Love is giving. God is love. God proved His love not by His need of us, but by His giving to us.

For God so loved the world, that He gave His only begotten Son, that whosoever

*believeth in Him should not perish, but
have everlasting life (John 3:16).*

> *Clinging to people is far
> different from loving them.*

The Scriptures plainly show that this infirmed woman had tried to lift herself. People
who stand on the outside can easily criticize and
assume that the infirmed woman lacks effort
and fortitude. That is not always the case. Some
situations in which we can find ourselves defy
will power. We feel unable to change. The Scriptures say that she "could in no wise lift up herself." That implies she had employed various
means of self-ministry. Isn't it amazing how the
same people who lift up countless others, often
cannot lift themselves? This type of person may
be a tower of faith and prayer for others, but im-
potent when it comes to her own limitations.
That person may be the one others rely upon.
Sometimes we esteem others more important
than ourselves. We always become the martyr. It
is wonderful to be self-sacrificing, but watch out
for self-disdain! If we don't apply some of the
medicine that we use on others to strengthen
ourselves, our patients will be healed and we
will be dying.

I shall not die, but live, and declare the works of the Lord (Psalm 118:17).

Many things can engender disappointment and depression. In this woman's case, a spirit of infirmity had gripped her life. A spirit can manifest itself in many forms. For some it may be low self-esteem caused by child abuse, rape, wife abuse or divorce. I realize that these are natural problems, but they are rooted in spiritual ailments. One of the many damaging things that can affect us today is divorce, particularly among women, who often look forward to a happy relationship. Little girls grow up playing with Barbie and Ken dolls, dressing doll babies and playing house. Young girls lie in bed reading romance novels, while little boys play ball and ride bicycles in the park. Whenever a woman is indoctrinated to think success is romance and then experiences the trauma of a failed relationship, she comes to a painful awakening. Divorce is not merely separating; it is the tearing apart of what was once joined together. Whenever something is torn, it does not heal easily. But Jesus can heal a broken or torn heart!

The Spirit of the Lord is upon Me, because He hath anointed Me to preach the gospel to the poor; He hath sent Me to heal the brokenhearted, to preach deliverance to the captives, and recovering of sight to the blind, to set at liberty them that are bruised (Luke 4:18).

Approximately five out of ten marriages end in divorce. Those broken homes leave a trail of broken dreams, people, and children. Only the Master can heal these victims in the times in which we live. He can treat the long-term effects of this tragedy. One of the great healing balms of the Holy Spirit is forgiveness. To forgive is to break the link between you and your past. Sadly enough, many times the person hardest to forgive is the one in the mirror. Although they rage loudly about others, people secretly blame themselves for a failed relationship.

> *To forgive is to break the link between you and your past.*

Regardless of who you hold responsible, there is no healing in blame! When you begin to realize that your past does not necessarily dictate the outcome of your future, then you can release the hurt. It is impossible to inhale new air until you exhale the old. I pray that as you continue reading, God would give the grace of releasing where you have been so you can receive what God has for you now. Exhale, then inhale; there is more for you.

Perhaps one of the more serious indictments against our civilization is our flagrant disregard for the welfare of our children. Child abuse, regardless of whether it is physical, sexual or emotional, is a terrible issue for an innocent mind to wrestle with. It is horrifying to think that little children who survive the peril of the streets, the public schools and the aggravated society in which we live, come home to be abused in what should be a haven. Recent statistics suggest that three in five young girls in this country have been or will be sexually assaulted. If that many are reported, I shudder to think of those that never are reported but are covered with a shroud of secrecy.

If by chance you are a pastor, please realize that these figures are actually faces in your choir, committees, etc. They reflect a growing amount of our congregational needs. Although this book focuses on women, many men also have been abused as children. I fear that God will judge us for our blatant disregard of this need in our messages, ministries, and prayers. I even would suggest that our silence contributes to the shame and secrecy that satan attaches to these victimized persons.

Whenever I think on these issues, I am reminded of what my mother used to say. I was forever coming home with a scratch or cut from schoolyard play. My mother would take the band-aid off, clean the wound and say, "Things that are covered don't heal well." Mother was right. Things that are covered do not heal well.

> *Things that are covered do not heal well.*

Perhaps Jesus was thinking on this order when He called the infirmed woman to come forward. It takes a lot of courage even in church today to receive ministry in sensitive areas. The Lord, though, is the kind of physician who can pour on the healing oil. Uncover your wounds in His presence and allow Him to gently heal the injuries. One woman found healing in the hem of His garment (Mark 5:25-29). There is a balm in Gilead! (Jer. 8:22).

Even when the victim survives, there is still a casualty. It is the death of trust. Surely you realize that little girls tend to be trusting and unsuspicious. When those who should nurture and protect them violate that trust through illicit behavior, multiple scars result. It is like programming a computer with false information;

you can get out of it only what has been programmed into it.

When a man tells a little girl that his per-
verted acts are normal, she has no reason not to
believe that what she is being taught is true.
She is devoted to him, allowing him to fondle
her or further misappropriate his actions toward her. Usually the abuser is someone very
close, with access to the child at vulnerable
times. Fear is also a factor, as many children lay
down with the cold taste of fear in their mouths.
They believe he could and would kill them for
divulging his liberties against them. Some, as
the victims of rape, feel physically powerless to
wrestle with the assailant.

What kind of emotions might this kind of
conduct bring out in the later life of this person?
I am glad you asked. It would be easy for this
kind of little girl to grow into a young lady who
has difficulty trusting anyone! Maybe she learns
to deal with the pain inside by getting attention
in illicit ways. Drug rehabilitation centers and
prisons are full of adults who were abused children needing attention.

Not every abused child takes such drastic
steps. Often their period of behavioral disorder
dissipates with time. However, the abused child
struggles with her own self-worth. She reasons,
"How can I be valuable if the only way I could

please my own father was to have sex with him?" This kind of childhood can affect how later relationships progress. Intimidated by intimacy, she struggles with trusting anyone. Insecurity and jealousy may be constant companions to this lady, who can't seem to grasp the idea that someone could love her. There are a variety of reactions as varied as there are individuals. Some avoid people who really care, being attracted to those who do not treat them well. Relating to abuse, they seem to sabotage good relationships and struggle for years in worthless ones. Still others may be emotionally incapacitated to the degree that they need endless affirmation and affection just to maintain the courage to face ordinary days.

The pastor may tell this lady that God is her heavenly Father. That doesn't help, because the problem is her point of reference. We frame our references around our own experiences. If those experiences are distorted, our ability to comprehend spiritual truths can be off center. I know that may sound very negative for someone who is in that circumstance. What do you do when you have been poorly programmed by life's events? I've got good news! You can re-program your mind through the Word of God.

Do not conform any longer to the pattern of this world, but be transformed by the renewing of your mind. Then you will be able to test and approve what God's will is—His good, pleasing and perfect will (Romans 12:2 NIV)

The Greek word metamorphôo is translated as "transformed" in this text. Literally, it means to change into another form! You can have a complete metamorphosis through the Word of God. It has been my experience as a pastor who does extensive counseling in my own ministry and abroad, that many abused people, women in particular, tend to flock to legalistic churches who see God primarily as a disciplinarian. Many times the concept of fatherhood for them is a harsh code of ethics. This type of domineering ministry may appeal to those who are performance-oriented. I understand that morality is important in Christianity; however, there is a great deal of difference between morality and legalism. It is important that God not be misrepresented. He is a balanced God, not an extremist.

The Word became flesh and made His dwelling among us. We have seen His glory, the glory of the One and Only, who came from the Father, full of grace and truth (John 1:14 NIV).

The glory of God is manifested only when there is a balance between grace and truth. Religion doesn't transform. Legalism doesn't transform. For the person who feels dirty, harsh rules could create a sense of self-righteousness. God doesn't have to punish you to heal you. Jesus has already prayed for you.

> *The glory of God is manifested only when there is a balance between grace and truth.*

Sanctify them through Thy truth: Thy word is truth (John 17:17).

Jesus simply shared grace and truth with that hurting woman. He said, "Woman, thou art loosed." Believe the Word of God and be free. Jesus our Lord was a great emancipator of the oppressed. It does not matter whether someone has been oppressed socially, sexually or racially; our Lord is an eliminator of distinctions.

There is neither Jew nor Greek [racial], *there is neither bond nor free* [social], *there is neither male nor female* [sexual]: *for ye are all one in Christ Jesus* (Galatians 3:28).

I feel it is important to point out that this verse deals with unity and equality in regard to the covenant of salvation. That is to say, God is no respecter of persons. He tears down barriers that would promote prejudice and separation in the Body of Christ. Yet it is important also to note that while there is no distinction in the manner in which we receive any of those groups, there should be an appreciation for the uniqueness of the groups' individuality. There is a racial, social and sexual uniqueness that we should not only accept, but also appreciate. It is cultural rape to teach other cultures or races that the only way to worship God is the way another race or culture does. Unity should not come at the expense of uniqueness of expression. We should also tolerate variance in social classes. It is wonderful to teach prosperity as long as it is understood that the Church is not an elite organization for spiritual yuppies only— one that excludes other social classes.

If uniqueness is to be appreciated racially and socially, it is certainly to be appreciated sexually. Male and female are one in Christ. Yet they are unique and that uniqueness is not to be tampered with. Let the male be masculine and the female be feminine! It is a sin for a man to misrepresent himself by conducting himself as a woman. I am not merely speaking of homosexuality. I am also talking about men who are feminine in their mannerisms. Many of these men may not be homosexual in their behavior, but the Bible says that they must be healed of feminine mannerisms, or vice versa. It is equally sad to see a masculine woman. Nevertheless, God wants them healed, not hated!

> *Know ye not that the unrighteous shall not inherit the kingdom of God? Be not deceived: neither fornicators, nor idolaters, nor adulterers, nor effeminate, nor abusers of themselves with mankind....* (1 Corinthians 6:9).

Strong's #3120 "*malakos* (mal-ak-os'); of uncertain affinity; soft, i.e. fine (clothing); figuratively, a catamite:—effeminate, soft" (*Strong's Exhaustive Concordance of the Bible*, Hendrickson Publishers, n.d.).

I realize that these behavioral disorders are areas that require healing and prayer. My point is simply that unity does not negate uniqueness. God is saying, "I don't want men to lose their masculine uniqueness." This is true racially, socially, and sexually. God can appreciate our differences and still create unity. It is like a conductor who can orchestrate extremely different instruments into producing a harmonious, unified sound. Together we produce a sound of harmony that expresses the multifaceted character of God.

Unity does not negate uniqueness.

Having established the uniqueness of unity, let us now discuss some aspects of the uniqueness of the woman. By nature a woman is a receiver. She is not physically designed to be a giver. Her sexual and emotional fulfillment becomes somewhat dependent on the giving of her male counterpart (in regard to intimate relationships). There is a certain vulnerability that is a part of being a receiver. In regard to reproduction (sexual relationships), the man is the contributing factor, and the woman is the receiver.

What is true of the natural is true of the spiritual. Men tend to act out of what they perceive to be facts, while women tend to react out of their emotions. If your actions and moods are not a reaction to the probing of the Holy Spirit, then you are reacting to the subtle taunting of the enemy. He is trying to produce his destructive fruit in your home, heart, and even in your relationships. Receiver, be careful what you receive! Moods and attitudes that satan would offer, you need to resist. Tell the enemy, "This is not me, and I don't receive it." It is his job to offer it and your job to resist it. If you do your job, all will go well.

Submit yourselves, then, to God. Resist the devil, and he will flee from you (James 4:7 NIV).

Don't allow the enemy to plug into you and violate you through his subtle seductions. He is a giver and he is looking for a receiver. You must discern his influence if you are going to rebuke him. Anything that comes, any mood that is not in agreement with God's Word, is satan trying to plug into the earthly realm through your life. He wants you to believe you cannot change. He loves prisons and chains! Statements like, "This is just the way I am," or "I am in a terrible mood today," come from lips that accept what they ought to reject. Never allow yourself to settle for anything less than the attitude God wants you to have in your heart. Don't let satan have your day, your husband, or your home. Eve could have put the devil out!

> *Statements like, "This is just the way I am," or "I am in a terrible mood today," come from lips that accept what they ought to reject.*

Neither give place to the devil (Eph.4:27).

It is not enough to reject the enemy's plan. You must nurture the Word of the Lord. You need to draw the promise of God and the vision for the future to your breast. It is a natural law that anything not fed will die. Whatever you have drawn to the breast is what is growing in your life. Breastfeeding holds several advantages for what you feed: (a) It hears your heartbeat; (b) it is warmed by your closeness; (c) it draws nourishment from you. Caution: Be sure you are nurturing what you want to grow and starving what you want to die.

> *Be sure you are nurturing what you want to grow and starving what you want to die.*

As you read this, you may feel that life is passing you by. You often experience success in one area and gross defeat in others. You need a burning desire for the future, the kind of desire that overcomes past fear and inhibitions. You will remain chained to your past and all the secrets therein until you decide: Enough is enough! I am telling you that when your desire for the future peaks, you can break out of prison. I challenge you to sit down and write 30 things you would like to do with your life and scratch them off, one by one, as you accomplish them. There is no way you can plan for the future and dwell in the past at the same time. I feel an earthquake coming into your prison! It is midnight—the turning point of days! It is your time for a change. Praise God and escape out of the dungeons of your past.

> *And at midnight Paul and Silas prayed, and sang praises unto God: and the prisoners heard them. And suddenly there was a great earthquake, so that the foundations of the prison were shaken: and immediately all the doors were opened, and every one's bands were loosed* (Acts 16:25-26)

Have you ever noticed how hard it is to communicate with people who will not give you their attention? Pain will not continue to rehearse itself in the life of a preoccupied, distracted person. Distracted people almost seem weird. They do not respond! Every woman has something she wishes she could forget. There is a principle to learn here. Forgetting isn't a memory lapse; it is a memory release! Like carbon dioxide the body can no longer use, exhale it and let it go out of your spirit.

> *Brethren, I count not myself to have apprehended: but this one thing I do, forgetting those things which are behind, and reaching forth unto those things which are before, I press toward the mark for the prize of the high calling of God in Christ Jesus. Let us therefore, as many*

*as be perfect, be thus minded: and if in
any thing ye be otherwise minded, God
shall reveal even this unto you* (Philippians 3:13-15).

Jesus set the infirmed woman free. She was able to stand upright. The crippling condition of her infirmity was removed by the God who cares, sees and calls the infirmity to the dispensary of healing and deliverance. You can call upon Him even in the middle of the night. Like a 24-hour medical center, you can reach Him at anytime. He is touched by the feeling of your infirmity.

*For we have not an high priest which
cannot be touched with the feeling of
our infirmities; but was in all points
tempted like as we are, yet without sin*
(Hebrews 4:15).

In the name of our High Priest, Jesus Christ, I curse the infirmity that has bowed the backs of God's women. I pray that, as we share together out of the Word of God, the Holy Spirit would roll you into the recovery room where you can fully realize that the trauma is over. I am excited to say that God never loosed anybody that He wasn't going to use mightily. May God reveal healing and purpose as we continue to seek Him.

Thoughts and Reflections

_____

_____

_____

_____

_____

_____

_____

_____

_____

_____

_____

_____

_____

_____

_____

_____

_____

_____

_____

_____

_____

_____

_____

_____

Infirmed Woman

_____

_____

_____

_____

_____

_____

_____

_____

_____

_____

_____

_____

_____

_____

_____

_____

_____

_____

_____

_____

_____

Infirmed Woman

The Transformers

*B*ut *as many as received Him, to them gave He power to become the sons of God, even to them that believe on His name* (John 1:12).

I pray that we as Christians never lose our conviction that God does change lives. We must protect this message. Our God enables us to make the radical changes necessary for fulfilling our purposes and responsibilities. Like the caterpillar that eats and sleeps its way into change, the process occurs gradually, but nonetheless powerfully. Many people who will rock this world are sleeping in the cocoon of obscurity, waiting for their change to come. The Scriptures declare, "...it is high time to awake out of sleep: for now is our salvation nearer than when we believed" (Rom. 13:11).

A memory of my twin sons playing on the floor when they were children tailors the continuity of this text for me. They were playing with a truck, contributing all the sounds of grinding gears and roaring engines. I didn't pay much attention as I began unwinding from the day's stresses and challenges. Distractedly, I glanced down at the floor and noticed that the boys were now running an airplane down an imaginary runway. I asked, "What happened to the truck you were playing with?" They explained, "Daddy, this is a transformer!" I then inquired, "What is a transformer?" Their answer brought me into the Presence of the Lord. They said, "It can be transformed from what it was before into whatever we want it to be!"

Suddenly I realized that God had made the first transformer! He created man from dust. He created him in such a way that, if need be, He could pull a woman out of him without ever having to reach back into the dust. Out of one creative act God transformed the man into a marriage. Then He transformed the marriage into a family, the family into a society, etc. God never had to reach into the ground again because the power to transform was intrinsically placed into man. All types of potential were locked into our spirits before birth. For the Christian, transformation at its optimum is the outworking of the internal. God placed certain things in us that must come out. We house the prophetic power of God. Every word of our personal prophetic destiny is inside us. He has ordained us to be!

> *Before I formed thee in the belly I knew thee; and before thou camest forth out of the womb I sanctified thee, and I ordained thee a prophet unto the nations* (Jeremiah 1:5).

Only when we are weary from trying to unlock our own resources do we come to the Lord, receive Him, and allow Him to release in us the power to become whatever we need to be. Actually, isn't that what we want to know: our purpose? Then we can use the power to become who we really are. Life has chiseled many of us into mere fragments of who we were meant to be. To all who receive Him, Christ gives the power to slip out of who they were forced into being so they can transform into the individual they each were created to be.

Salvation as it relates to destiny is the God-given power to become what God has eternally decreed you were before. "Before what?" you ask; before the foundation of the world. What Christians so often refer to as grace truly is God's divine enablement to accomplish predestined purpose. When the Lord says to Paul, "My grace is sufficient for thee..." (2 Cor. 12:9), He is simply stating that His power is not intimidated by your circumstances. You are empowered by God to reach and accomplish goals that transcend human limitations! It is important that each and every vessel God uses realize that they were able to accomplish what others could not only because God gave them the grace to do so. Problems are not really problems to a person who has the grace to serve in a particular area.

> *Remember, God always empowers whomever He employs.*

How many times have people walked up to me and said, "I don't see how you can stand this or that." If God has given us the grace to operate in a certain situation, those things do not affect us as they would someone else who does not have the grace to function in that area. Therefore, it is important that we not imitate other people. Assuming that we may be equally talented, we still may not be equally graced. Remember, God always empowers whomever He employs. Ultimately, we must realize that the excellency of our gifts are of God and not of us. He doesn't need nearly as much of our contributions as we think He does. So it is God who works out the internal destinies of men. He gives us the power to become who we are eternally and internally.

> *Wherefore, my beloved, as ye have always obeyed, not as in my presence only, but now much more in my absence, work out your own salvation with fear and trembling. For it is God which worketh in you both to will and to do of His good pleasure* (Philippians 2:12-13).

Today in the Body of Christ a great deal of emphasis is placed on the process of mentoring. The concept of mentoring is both scriptural and effective; however, as we often do, many of us have gone to extremes. Instead of teaching young men to pursue God, the ultimate Rabbi, they are running amuck looking for a man to pour into them. All men are not mentored as Joshua was—under the firm hand of a strong leader. Some, like Moses, are prepared by the workings of the manifold wisdom of God. This latter group receives mentoring through the carefully orchestrated circumstances that God ordains to accomplish an end result. Regardless of which describes your ascent to greatness, it is still God who "worketh in you both to will and to do." When you understand this, you appreciate the men or the methods God used, but ultimately praise the God whose masterful ability to conduct has crescendoed in the finished product of a man or woman of God.

And the Lord said unto Moses, Gather unto Me seventy men of the elders of Israel, whom thou knowest to be the elders of the people, and officers over them; and bring them unto the tabernacle of the congregation, that they may stand there with thee (Numbers 11:16).

In keeping with this mentoring concept, let's consider Moses' instructions when asked to consecrate elders in Israel. I found it interesting that God told Moses to gather unto Him men whom he knew were elders. God says, "I want you to separate men to be elders who are elders." You can only ordain a man to be what he already is. The insight we need to succeed is the discernment of who is among us. Woe unto the man who is placed into what he is not. Moses was to bring these men into a full circle. In other words, they were to be led into what they already were. Perhaps this will further clarify my point: When the prodigal son was in the "hog pen," it was said, "And when he came to himself…" (Luke 15:17). We are fulfilled only when we are led into being who we were predestined to be. Real success is coming to ourselves.

The thing that gives a man power to arise above his circumstances is his coming to himself. You feel fulfilled when you achieve a sense of belonging through your job, family, or ministry. Have you ever met anyone who left you with a feeling of familiarity—almost as if you had known the person? A sense of bonding comes out of similarities. Likewise, there are certain jobs or ministries that feel comfortable, even if they are tasks you have never done before. If you are discerning, you can feel a sense of belonging in certain situations. However, weary are the legs of a traveler who cannot find his way home. Spiritual wanderings plague the lives of many people who wrestle with discontentment. May God grant you success in finding your way to a sense of wholeness and completion.

Change is a gift from God. It is given to the person who finds himself too far removed from what he feels destiny has ordained for him. There is nothing wrong with being wrong-but there is something wrong with not making the necessary adjustments to get things right!

Even within the Christian community, some do not believe in God's ability to change the human heart. This unbelief in God's ability to change causes people to judge others on the basis of their past. Dead issues are periodically revived in the mouths of gossips. Still, the Lord progressively regenerates the mind of His children. Don't assume that real change occurs without struggle and prayer. However, change can be achieved.

God exalted Him to His own right hand as Prince and Savior that He might give repentance and forgiveness of sins to Israel (Acts 5:31 NIV).

The Bible calls change repentance. Repentance is God's gift to a struggling heart who wants to find himself. The Lord wants to bring you to a place of safety and shelter. Without the Holy Spirit's help you can search and search and still not find repentance. The Lord will show the place of repentance only to those who hunger and thirst after righteousness. One moment with the Spirit of God can lead you into a place of renewal that, on your own, you would not find or enjoy. I believe it was this kind of grace that made John Newton record, "It was grace that taught my heart to fear and grace my fears relieved. How precious did that grace appear the hour I first believed" (Amazing Grace, early American melody). When God gives you the grace to make changes that you know you couldn't do with your own strength, it becomes precious to you.

> *For ye know how that afterward, when he would have inherited the blessing, he was rejected: for he found no place of repentance, though he sought it carefully with tears* (Hebrews 12:17).

Brother Esau sought for the place of repentance and could not secure it. To be transformed is to be changed. If you are not moving into your divine purpose, you desperately need to repent. "Repent" has a strong negative connotation for the person indoctrinated to be-lieve that repentance is a fearful and dangerous action. It is not dangerous. Repentance is the prerequisite of revival. There cannot be revival without prayerful repentance. John the Baptist taught Israel, "Repent ye: for the kingdom of Heaven is at hand" (Matt. 3:2). If God wants you to change, it is because He wants you to be prepared for what He desires to do next in your life. Get ready; the best is yet to come.

> *Repentance is the prerequisite of revival.*

For whom He did foreknow, He also did predestinate to be conformed to the image of His Son, that He might be the firstborn among many brethren (Romans 8:29).

And be not conformed to this world: but be ye transformed by the renewing of your mind, that ye may prove what is that good, and acceptable, and perfect, will of God (Romans 12:2).

Now let's deal with some real issues! The word *conformed* in Romans 8:29 is *summorphoo* (Strong's #4832), which means "to be fashioned like or shaped into the image or the picture" of—in this case—Christ. God has predestined you to shape up into a picture of Christ in the earth. Christ is the firstborn of a huge family of siblings who all bear a striking resemblance to their Father. The shaping of a will, however, requires a visit to the Garden of Gethsemane. *Gethsemane* literally means oil press (Strong's #1068). God presses the oil of His anointing out of your life through adversity. When you forsake your will in order to be shaped into a clearer picture of Christ, you will see little drops of oil coming out in your walk and work for God. In short, He predestined the pressing in your life that produces the oil. As you are pressed, you gradually conform to the image of your predestined purpose.

In Romans 12:2 we are instructed not to be conformed to this world. Literally, it says we are not to be conformed to the same pattern of this world. The text warns us against submitting to the dictates of the world. We are to avoid using those standards as a pattern for our progress. On a deeper level God is saying, "Do not use the same pattern of the world to measure success or to establish character and values." The term *world* in Greek is *aion* (Strong's #165), which refers to ages. Together these words tell us, "Do not allow the pattern of the times you are in to become the pattern that shapes your inward person."

At this point I can almost hear someone saying, "How do you respond to the preexisting circumstances and conditions that have greatly affected you?" Or, "I am already shaped into something less than what God would want me to be because of the times in which I live or the circumstances in which I grew up." I am glad you asked these things. You see, every aspect of your being that has already been conformed to this age must be transformed! The prefix *trans-* implies movement, as in the words *transport, translate, transact, transition*, etc. In this light, transform would imply moving the form. On a deeper level it means moving from one form into another, as in the tadpole that is transformed into the frog, and the caterpillar into the butterfly. No matter what has disfigured you, in God is the power to be transformed.

Many individuals in the Body of Christ are persevering without progressing. They wrestle with areas that have been conformed to the world instead of transformed. This is particularly true of us Pentecostals who often emphasize the gifts of the Spirit and exciting services. It is imperative that, while we keep our mode of expression, we understand that transformation doesn't come from inspiration! Many times preachers sit down after ministering a very inspiring sermon feeling that they accomplished more than they actually did. Transformation takes place in the mind.

The Bible teaches that we are to be renewed by the transforming of our minds (see Rom. 12:2; Eph. 4:23). Only the Holy Spirit knows how to renew the mind. The struggle we have inside us is with our self-perception. Generally our perception of ourselves is affected by those around us. Our early opinion of ourselves is deeply affected by the opinions of the authoritative figures in our formative years. If our parents tend to neglect or ignore us, it tears at our self-worth. Eventually, though, we mature to the degree where we can walk in the light of our own self-image, without it being diluted by the contributions of others.

When we experience the new birth, we again go back to the formative years of being deeply impressionable. It's important to be discerning in who we allow to influence us in the early years. Whenever we become intimate with someone, the first thing we should want to know is, "Who do you say that I am?" Our basic need is to be understood by the inner circle of people with whom we walk. However, we must be ready to abort negative, destructive information that doesn't bring us into an accelerated awareness of inner realities and strengths. Jesus was able to ask Peter, "Who do you say that I am?" because He already knew the answer! (See Matthew 16:15). To ask someone to define you without first knowing the answer within yourself is dangerous. When we ask that kind of question, without an inner awareness, we open the door for manipulation. In short, Jesus knew who He was.

The Lord wants to help you realize who you are and what you are graced to do. When you understand that He is the only One who really knows you, then you pursue Him with fierceness and determination. Pursue Him! Listen to what Paul shares at the meeting on Mars' Hill.

And hath made of one blood all nations of men for to dwell on all the face of the earth, and hath determined the times before appointed, and the bounds of their habitation; that they should seek the Lord, if haply they might feel after Him, and find Him, though He be not far from every one of us: for in Him we live, and move, and have our being; as certain also of your own poets have said, For we are also His offspring (Acts 17:26-28).

The basic message of this passage is that God has set the bounds on our habitations. He knows who we are and how we are to attain. This knowledge, locked up in the counsel of God's omniscience, is the basis of our pursuit, and it is the release of that knowledge that brings immediate transformation. He knows the hope or the goal of our calling. He is not far removed from us; He reveals Himself to people who seek Him. The finders are the seekers. The door is opened only to the knockers and the gifts are given to the askers! (See Luke 11:9.) Initiation is our responsibility. Whosoever hungers and thirsts shall be filled. Remember, in every crisis He is never far from the seeker!

Transforming truths are brought forth through the birth canal of our diligence in seeking His face. It is while you are in His presence that He utters omniscient insights into your individual purpose and course. Jesus told a woman who had been wrestling with a crippling condition for 18 years that she was not really bound-that in fact she was loosed! Immediately she was transformed by the renewing of her mind. (See Luke 13:11-13.) It is no wonder David said, "In Thy presence is fulness of joy" (Ps. 16:11b). The answer is in the Presence-the Presence of God, not man! There is a renewing word that will change your mind about your circumstance. Just when the enemy thinks he has you, transform before his very eyes!

No matter who left his impression upon you, God's Word prevails! The obstacles of past scars can be overcome by present truths. Your deliverance will not start in your circumstances; it will always evolve out of your mentality. As the Word of God waxes greater, the will of men becomes weaker. Paul said in Ephesians 5:26 that Jesus cleanses by the "washing of water by the word." So turn the faucet on high and ease your mind down into the sudsy warm water of profound truth. Gently wash away every limitation and residue of past obstacles and gradually, luxuriously, transform into the refreshed, renewed person you were created to become. Whenever someone tells you what you can't do or be, or what you can't get or attain, then tell them, "I can do all things through Christ who strengthens me! I am a transformer!"

> *Your deliverance will not start in your circumstances; it will always evolve out of your mentality.*

Thoughts and Reflections

_____

_____

_____

_____

_____

_____

_____

_____

_____

_____

_____

_____

_____

_____

_____

_____

_____

_____

_____

_____

_____

_____

_____

_____

_____

_____

_____
_____
_____
_____
_____
_____
_____
_____
_____
_____
_____
_____
_____
_____
_____
_____
_____
_____
_____
_____
_____
_____
_____
_____

The Transformers

_____

_____

_____

_____

_____

_____

_____

_____

_____

_____

_____

_____

_____

_____

_____

_____

_____

_____

_____

_____

_____

_____

_____

The Fear of the Father

Have you ever tasted that cold, acid-like taste of fear? I mean the kind of fear that feels like a cinder block is being dragged across the pit of your stomach. It's the kind where cold chills trimmed with a prickly sensation flood your body, adorning itself in a distinct sense of nausea. No matter how strong we are, there is always something that can cause the heart to flutter and the pulse to weaken.

Fear is as lethal to us as paralysis of the brain. It makes our thoughts become arthritic and our memory sluggish. It is the kind of feeling that can make a graceful person stumble up the stairs in a crowd. You know what I mean—the thing that makes the articulate stutter and the rhythmic become spastic. Like an oversized growth, fear soon becomes impossible to camouflage. Telltale signs like trembling knees or quivering lips betray fear even in the most disciplined person. Fear is the nightmare of the stage; it haunts the hearts of the timid as well as of the intimidated.

From the football field to the ski slope, fear has a visa or entrance that allows it to access the most discriminating crowd. It is not prejudiced, nor is it socially conscious. It can attack the impoverished or the aristocratic. When it grips the heart of a preacher, his notes turn into a foreign language and his breathing becomes asthmatic.

To me, there is no fear like the fear of the innocent. This is the fear of a child who walks into a dark basement to find the light switch far from reach—and every mop and bucket becomes a sinister, sleazy creature whose cold breath lurks upon the neck of life's little apprentice. I can remember moments as a child when I thought my heart had turned into an African tom-tom that was being beaten by an insane musician whose determined beating would soon break through my chest like the bursting of a flood-engorged dam.

Even now I can only speculate how long it took for fear to give way to normalcy, or for the distant rumble of a racing heart to recede into the steadiness of practical thinking and rationality. I can't estimate time because fear traps time and holds it hostage in a prison of icy anxiety. Eventually, though, like the thawing of icicles on the roof of an aged and sagging house, my heart would gradually melt into a steady and less pronounced beat.

I confess that maturity has chased away many of the ghosts and goblins of my youthful closet of fear. Nevertheless, there are still those occasional moments when reason gives way to the fanciful imagination of the fearful little boy in me, who peeks his head out of my now fully developed frame like a turtle sticks his head out of its shell with caution and precision.

The Love of the Father

My little children, of whom I travail in birth again until Christ be formed in you (Galatians 4:19).

Thank God that He understands the hidden part within each of us. He understands the child in us, and He speaks to our blanket-clutching, thumb-sucking infantile need. In spite of our growth, income, education, or notoriety, He still speaks to the childhood issues of the aging heart. This is the ministry that only a Father can give.

Have you ever noticed that you are never a grown-up to the ones who birthed you? They completely disregard the gray hairs, crowfeet, and bulging, blossoming waistlines of abundant life. No matter how many children call you "Dad" or "Mom," to your parents you are still just a child yourself. They seem to think you have slipped into the closet to put on grown-up clothes and are really just playing a game. They must believe that somewhere beneath the receding hairline there is still a child, hiding in the darkness of adulthood. The worst part about it is (keep this quiet), I think they are right!

The Lord looks beyond our facade and sees the trembling places in our lives. He knows our innermost needs. No matter how spiritually mature we try to appear, He is still aware that lurking in the shadows is a discarded candy wrapper from the childish desire we just prayed off last night—the lingering evidence of some little temper or temptation that only the Father can see hiding within His supposedly "all grown-up" little child.

It is He alone whom we must trust to see the very worst in us, yet still think the very best of us. It is simply the love of a Father. It is the unfailing love of a Father whose son should have been old enough to receive his inheritance without acting like a child, without wandering off into failure and stumbling down the mine shaft of lasciviousness. Nevertheless, the Father's love throws a party for the prodigal and prepares a feast for the foolish. Comprehend with childhood faith the love of the Father we have in God!

When the disciples asked Jesus to teach them to pray, the first thing He taught them was to acknowledge the *fatherhood* of God. When we say "Our Father," we acknowledge His fatherhood and declare our sonship. Sonship is the basis for our relationship with Him as it relates to the privilege of belonging to His divine family. Similarly, one of the first words most babies say is "Daddy." So knowing your father helps you understand your own identity as a son or daughter. Greater still is the need to know not only *who* my father is, but *how he feels about me.*

It is not good to deny a child the right to feel his father's love. In divorce cases, some women use the children to punish their ex-husbands. Because of her broken covenant with the child's father, the mother may deny him the right to see his child. This is not good for the child! Every child is curious about his father.

Philip saith unto Him, Lord, show us the Father, and it sufficeth us (John 14:8).

Philip didn't know who the Father was, but he longed to see Him. I can still remember what it was like to fall asleep watching television and have my father pick up my listless, sleep-ridden frame from the couch and carry me up the stairs to bed. I would wake up to the faint smell of his "Old Spice" cologne and feel his strong arms around me, carrying me as if I weighed nothing at all. I never felt as safe and protected as I did in the arms of my father—that is, until he died and I was forced to seek refuge in the arms of my heavenly Father.

What a relief to learn that God can carry the load even better than my natural father could, and that He will never leave me nor forsake me! Perhaps it was this holy refuge that inspired the hymnist to pen the hymn, "What a fellowship, what a joy divine. Leaning on the everlasting arms" (from the lyrics of "Leaning on the Everlasting Arms," Elisha A. Hoffman, 1887).

Fear or Respect?

And unto man He said, Behold, the fear of the Lord, that is wisdom; and to depart from evil is understanding (Job 28:28).

The Hebrew term for "fear" in this verse is *yir'ah*, according to *Strong's Exhaustive Concordance of the Bible.* It means a moral fear, or reverence. So what attitude should we have toward our heavenly Father? The Bible declares that we should have a strong degree of reverence for Him. But a distinction must be made here: There is a great deal of difference between fear and reverence.

The term *reverence* means to respect or revere; but the term *fear* carries with it a certain connotation of terror and intimidation. That kind of fear is not a healthy attitude for a child of God to have about his heavenly Father. The term rendered "fear" in Job 28:28 could be better translated as "respect." Fear will drive man away from God like it drove Adam to hide in the bushes at the sound of the voice of his only Deliverer. Adam said, "I heard Thy voice in the garden, and I was afraid..." (Gen. 3:10). That is not the reaction a loving father wants from his children. I don't want my children to scatter and hide like mice when I approach! I may not always agree with what they have done, but I will always love who they are.

I remember an occasion when some students from the elementary school my sons attended saw me for the first time. Because I stand a good 6'2" and weigh over 250 pounds, the little children were completely astonished. The other children told my sons, "Look at how big your dad is! I bet he would just about kill you. Aren't you afraid of him?" My sons quickly responded with glee, "Afraid of him? Nah, he's not mean. He's our dad!" They were not afraid of my stature because they were secure in our relationship. Does that mean they have never been punished? Of course not! What it does mean is they have never been abused! My love holds my judgment in balance.

As imperfect as I admit I am, if I know how to love my children, what about God? Oh friend, He may not approve of your conduct, but He still loves you! In fact, when you come to understand this fact, it will help you improve your conduct.

> *Or despisest thou the riches of His goodness and forbearance and longsuffering; not knowing that the goodness of God leadeth thee to repentance?* (Romans 2:4)

If this text is true (and it is), then we must tell of God's goodness to those who need to repent. I believe the Church has confused *conviction* with *condemnation*. The Holy Spirit convicts us of sin. *Conviction* leads us to a place of deliverance and change. *Condemnation* leads us to the gallows of despair and hopelessness.

I believe the Church has confused conviction with condemnation.

Why have we withheld from so many bleeding hearts the good news of the gospel? We have replaced this good news with the rambunctious ramblings of self-righteous rhetoric! I believe that we must assume the ministry of reconciliation and cause men to be reconciled back to their God.... We must remember that the only antidote is in the presence of the Lord....

> *Conviction leads us to a place of deliverance and change. Condemnation leads us to the gallows of despair and hopelessness.*

Thoughts and Reflections

_____

_____

_____

_____

_____

_____

_____

_____

_____

_____

_____

_____

_____

_____

_____

_____

_____

_____

_____

_____

_____

_____

Other Books, Videos, and Audiocassettes
by T.D. Jakes

Water in the Wilderness: God's Provision for Your Every Need

Just before you apprehend your greatest conquest, expect the greatest struggle. Many are perplexed who encounter this season of adversity. This book will show you how to survive the worst of times with the greatest of ease and will cause fountains of living water to spring out of the parched, sun-drenched areas in your life. This word is a refreshing stream in the desert for the weary traveler.

Why? Because You Are Anointed

Why do the righteous, who have committed their entire lives to obeying God, seem to endure so much pain and experience such conflict? These perplexing questions have plagued and bewildered Christians for ages. In this anointed and inspirational new book, Bishop T.D. Jakes, the preacher with the velvet touch and explosive delivery, provocatively and skillfully answers these questions and many more as well as answering the "Why" of the anointed.

Why? Workbook

Why? Workbook will help you to understand and overcome the difficulties that surround your own life. Over 150 thought-provoking questions will help you discover answers to the "whys" in your own life. Designed with a user-friendly, cutting-edge study system and answer key, it is an exciting and powerful tool for individual group studies.

Woman, Thou Art Loosed!

This book offers healing to hurting single mothers, insecure women, and battered wives.

Abused girls and women in crises are exchanging their despair for hope! Hurting women around the nation and those who minister to them are devouring the compassionate truths in Bishop T.D. Jakes' *Woman, Thou Art Loosed!* Also available as a workbook.

Can You Stand to Be Blessed?

Does any runner enter a race without training for it? Does a farmer expect a harvest without preparing a field? Do Christians believe they can hit the mark without taking aim? In this book, T.D. Jakes teaches you how to unlock the inner strength to go on in God. These practical scriptural principles will release you to fulfill your intended purpose. The only question that remains is, *Can You Stand to Be Blessed?*

Manpower—Healing the Wounded Man Within *(Audio Series)*

Wounded men will experience the transforming power of God's Word in *Manpower.* Satan has plotted to destroy the male, but God will literally raise up thousands of men through this life-changing, soul-cleansing, and mind-renewing word. This four-part audio series is for every man who ever had an issue he could not discuss; for every man who needed to bare his heart and had no one to hear it.

Get in the Birth Position—Inducing Your God-Inspired Dreams

God's Word is steadfast. Nothing can stop what God has promised from coming to pass. However, you need to get ready. In this message T.D. Jakes shares the steps necessary to bring to birth the promises of God in your life.

The 25th Hour—When God Stops Time For You! (Video)

Have you ever thought, "Lord, I need more time?" Joshua thought the same thing, and he called upon the sun and moon to stand still! This message from Joshua 10 testifies of the mightiness of our God, who can stop time and allow His children to accomplish His purposes and realize the victory!

The Puppet Master

The vastness of God, His omnipotence and omnipresence, His working in the spirit world— these are concepts difficult to grasp. In this anointed message, T.D. Jakes declares God's ability to work for your deliverance, for He can go where you cannot go, do what you cannot do, and reach what you cannot reach!

Tell the Devil "I Changed My Mind!"

The Scriptures declare that it is with the mind that we serve the Lord. If there was ever a battleground that satan wants to seize and dominate in your life, it's right in the arsenals of your own mind. We must get the victory in our thought-life.

I believe that even now God is calling every prodigal son back home. Both the lost and the lukewarm are being covered and clothed with His righteousness and grace. I pray that this life-changing, soul-cleansing, mind-renewing message will help you find your way from the pit back to the palace.

He Loved Me Enough to Be Late
—Delayed But Not Denied

Many of us have wondered, "God, what is taking You so long?" Often God doesn't do what we think He will, when we think He will, because He loves us. His love is willing to be criticized to accomplish its purpose. Jesus chose to wait until Lazarus had been dead for several days, and still raised him up! This message will challenge you to roll away your doubt and receive your miracle from the tomb!

Out of the Darkness Into the Light

When Jesus healed a blind man on the Sabbath by putting mud on his eyes and telling him to wash, He broke tradition in favor of deliverance. The Church must follow this example. Are we willing to move with God beyond some of the things we have come from? Can we look beyond our personal dark moments to God? The Light of the world is ready to burst into our lives!

When Shepherds Bleed

Shepherding is a dangerous profession, and no one knows that better than a pastor. Drawing from personal encounters with actual shepherds in Israel and years of ministry, Bishop T.D. Jakes and Stanley Miller provide unique insight into the hazards faced by pastors today. With amazing perception, the authors pull back the bandages and uncover the open, bleeding wounds common among those shepherding God's flock. Using the skills of spiritual surgeons, they precisely cut to the heart of the problem and tenderly apply the cure. You'll be moved to tears as your healing process begins. Open your heart and let God lead you beside the still waters where He can restore your soul.

The Harvest

Have you been sidetracked by satan? Are you preoccupied with the things of this world? Are you distracted by one crisis after another? You need to get your act together before it's too late! God's strategy for the end-time harvest is already set in motion. Phase One is underway, and Phase Two is close behind. If you don't want to be left out tomorrow, you need to take action today. With startling insight, T.D. Jakes sets the record straight. You'll be shocked to learn how God is separating people into two distinct categories. One thing is certain—after reading *The Harvest*, you'll know exactly where you stand with God. This book will help you discover who will and who won't be included in the final ingathering and determine what it takes to be prepared. If you miss *The Harvest*, you'll regret it for all eternity!

T.D. Jakes Ministries

P.O. Box 5390
Dallas, TX 75236
1-800-Bishop-2 (247-4672)